I'm Thinking of an African Animal

Bela Davis

Abdo Kids Junior
is an Imprint of Abdo Kids
abdobooks.com

Abdo
I'M THINKING OF AN ANIMAL
Kids

abdobooks.com

Published by Abdo Kids, a division of ABDO, P.O. Box 398166, Minneapolis, Minnesota 55439.

Printed in the United States of America, North Mankato, Minnesota.

052024

092024

THIS BOOK CONTAINS RECYCLED MATERIALS

Photo Credits: Shutterstock

Production Contributors: Teddy Borth, Jennie Forsberg, Grace Hansen

Design Contributors: Candice Keimig, Pakou Moua

Library of Congress Control Number: 2023948534

Publisher's Cataloging-in-Publication Data

Names: Davis, Bela, author.

Title: I'm thinking of an african animal / by Bela Davis

Description: Minneapolis, Minnesota : Abdo Kids, 2025 | Series: I'm thinking of an animal | Includes online resources and index.

Identifiers: ISBN 9798384900566 (lib. bdg.) | ISBN 9798384901266 (ebook) | ISBN 9798384901617 (Read-to-me eBook)

Subjects: LCSH: Big game animals--Africa--Juvenile literature. | Questions and answers--Juvenile literature. | Riddles--Juvenile literature. | Animals--Juvenile literature. | Zoology--Juvenile literature.

Classification: DDC 591.96--dc23

Table of Contents

Guess the Animal!

I'm thinking of an African animal. Can you guess what it is?

North America
Europe
Asia
Africa
South America
Australia

I'm thinking of an animal that lives in the **savanna**.

clues

- lives in the savanna

But it is not a giraffe!

I'm thinking of an animal that has four legs.

clues

- lives in the savanna
- has four legs

But it is not a lion!

I'm thinking of an animal that eats grass.

clues

- lives in the savanna
- has four legs
- eats grass

But it is not a zebra!

I'm thinking of an animal that lives in a group.

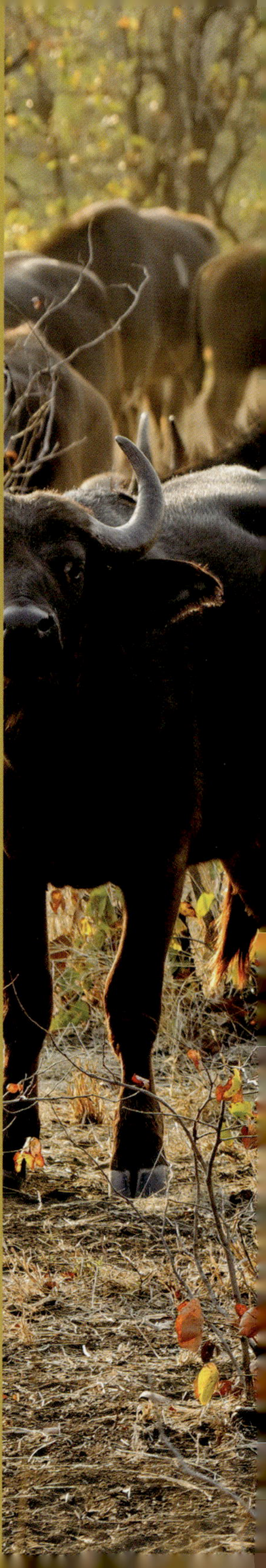

clues

- lives in the savanna
- has four legs
- eats grass
- lives in a group

But it is not an African buffalo!

I'm thinking of an animal that is gray in color.

clues

- lives in the savanna
- has four legs
- eats grass
- lives in a group
- is gray in color

But it is not a rhinoceros!

I'm thinking of an animal that has **tusks**.

clues

- lives in the savanna
- has four legs
- eats grass
- lives in a group
- is gray in color
- has tusks

But it is not an elephant!

Do you know what animal

I'm thinking of?

clues

- lives in the savanna
- has four legs
- eats grass
- lives in a group
- is gray in color
- has tusks

I'm thinking of a hippopotamus! Now it's your turn! What animal are you thinking of?

Comparing Animals

	giraffe	zebra	rhino	hippo
four legs	✓	✓	✓	✓
eats grass		✓	✓	✓
gray in color			✓	✓
tusks				✓

Glossary

savanna
a flat plain covered with grass that also has scattered trees. Savannas are found in Africa and other tropical regions.

tusk
a long, large, pointed tooth that sticks out from the mouth of some animals. Tusks grow in pairs and may be used to find food or fight.

Index